# The Road to Freedom

## Photographs and memorabil[?] the 1916 Rising an[?]

Michael Kenny

National Museum of Ireland

Published in 1993 by
Town House and Country House
42 Morehampton Road
Donnybrook
Dublin 4
Ireland

for The National Museum of Ireland

Text copyright © National Museum of Ireland, 1993

British Library Cataloguing in Publication Data. A catalogue record for this book is available from the British Library.

ISBN: 0-946172-35-8

*Acknowledgements*
The author and publishers would like to thank the following for permission to reproduce their photographs: The Ulster Museum for Photo 1 and Plate 4; Radio Telefís Éireann for Photos 6, 7, 9 and 49. All the other photographs belong to the National Museum of Ireland. Special thanks to Joseph Aylward, Margaret O'Shaughnessy and Anne Devenney of the National Museum, and to Oliver Snoddy and Mr F Glenn Thompson for their help.

Design: Bill Murphy
Origination: The Kulor Centre
Printed in Ireland by Criterion Press, Dublin

# CONTENTS

## INTRODUCTION

The Rising of 1916 and the War of Independence that followed in 1919–21 have had a profound influence on the shaping of modern Ireland. The disappearance of Home Rule from the political agenda, the Anglo-Irish Treaty of 1921, the Civil War of 1922–3, and the change in status from Free State to Republic in 1949, all had their roots in the momentous events of Easter week 1916.

The direct political background to 1916 must be sought in developments during the preceding decades and the failure of Britain to grant Home Rule to Ireland. The formation of the Ulster Volunteers in 1912 to oppose Home Rule, by arms if necessary, led directly to the establishment of the Irish Volunteers in 1913 to defend the measure. The latter were in turn infiltrated by the Irish Republican Brotherhood, whose aim was to make Ireland a Republic. The horrific living conditions of the urban working classes and the bitter strike and lock-out of 1913 were also important factors. The literary and cultural ferment of the period was significant too, and the formation of such organisations as the Gaelic Athletic Association (1884), the Gaelic League (1893) and Sinn Féin (1905), all contributed to the growth of a new atmosphere and to a spirit of self-reliance and freedom. There remained, admittedly, considerable disagreement between the various groups and personalities regarding the definition of that freedom and how it might be achieved. The shelving of Home Rule in 1914, however, and the outbreak of war, provided the catalyst that convinced the more determined revolutionaries that an armed uprising could succeed where previous attempts had failed.

The insurrection itself, although it caught the British authorities totally unawares, was not an unplanned rebellion of dreamers and poets as it has sometimes been portrayed. It was the result of painstaking planning, involving the Irish Republican Brotherhood, the Irish Volunteers, the Irish Citizen Army, Clan na Gael in America, and even imperial Germany, then at war with Britain. The capture of the German ammunition ship, the *Aud*, and the confusion that attended the mobilisation orders in the days leading up to Easter Monday 1916, destroyed any chance of success that the Rising might have had. The perception of it as a hopeless and foolhardy undertaking, however, is very much the wisdom of hindsight.

The aftermath of 1916 — the executions, internment, the dramatic change in public opinion and the intensification of guerilla warfare leading to the Truce of July 1921 — is well documented, and biographies of the major figures involved, such as Pádraig Pearse, James Connolly, Michael Collins and Éamon de Valera, have been published in recent years, so it is not intended to assess their contributions in detail here. The purpose of this book is to provide a general picture of the background to 1916, the Rising itself and its aftermath, illustrated with artefacts from the collections of the National Museum of Ireland. These collections, although extensive, have been formed over the years from donation, purchase and loan, resulting in some personalities and events being better represented than others. The material acquired includes flags, uniforms, guns, prison diaries, photographs and personal memorabilia relating to personalities and events of the period. As it is not possible to provide artefacts to illustrate every aspect of contemporary history, topics such as the opposition to conscription, the Black and Tans, and the handing over of power in 1922 are treated by means of contemporary photographs.

The time span covered here, beginning with the foundation of the Gaelic League in 1893 and ending with the Civil War of 1922–3, represents one of the most interesting periods in Irish history. It has been the source of discussion, controversy and disagreement among historians, academics and commentators. Regardless of how one interprets specific events or their significance, there can be no doubt that a knowledge of this period is crucial to understanding modern Ireland.

THE BACKGROUND

**The Fenian movement**
The republicans who took up arms in 1916 regarded themselves as direct

heirs to the republicanism of Wolfe Tone and the United Irishmen of the 1790s, the Young Irelanders of the 1840s and the Fenians of the 1860s. Indeed there was a direct and immediate link with the Fenian movement or Irish Republican Brotherhood (IRB). Founded in 1858, and pledged to the establishment of an Irish Republic, it survived as a secret society for over half a century, infiltrated most of the other nationalist movements, and provided the leadership and planning for the 1916 Rising. It had grown rapidly in strength and numbers not only in Ireland but also among Irish soldiers in the British Army and on both sides in the American Civil War. It was especially strong in the United States, under the name of the Fenian Brotherhood, but it was also active in Britain, Canada and Australia. Despite the organising genius of leaders such as James Stephens in Ireland and John O'Mahony in America, the movement was beset by internal rivalries, tension between the American and Irish wings, and a succession of British spies, some in senior positions.

A planned rising in 1865 never got off the ground, and most of the leaders in Ireland were arrested. An invasion of Canada from the United States by eight hundred men under General John O'Neill in 1866 was unsuccessful. An attempted rising in 1867 in Ireland was also unsuccessful, as was the last attempted invasion of Canada by the redoubtable General O'Neill in 1870. The execution of three Fenians in Manchester, who came to be known as the Manchester Martyrs, and growing sympathy for the plight of Fenian prisoners, helped to keep the movement alive however. Under the leadership of John Devoy, who reorganised the IRB, the 'New Departure' — a working alliance between the Fenians, the Land League and the Irish Parliamentary Party — took shape in 1879 and helped to change the course of Irish history. The Irish Parliamentary Party was led by the charismatic Charles Stewart Parnell and was dedicated to Home Rule for Ireland. The Land League, founded and led by Michael Davitt to defend the rights of tenants against the excessive demands of their landlords, included many IRB members in its ranks. The IRB therefore became increasingly involved in land agitation and political activity. Devoy's move had been shrewd. As Gladstone, the Liberal Prime Minister of Britain, admitted: 'With a political revolution we have ample strength to cope — but a social revolution is a very different matter.'

IRB members rose to positions of influence in the new sporting, cultural and political organisations that sprang up at the turn of the century. More importantly, the movement gained control of the Irish Volunteers, which led directly to the 1916 Rising. Since the birth of the Volunteers dates to the eve of the First World War, we will return to them a little later. Firstly, it is necessary to take a brief look at some of those organisations referred to above.

### The Gaelic League

The most radical of the cultural bodies was undoubtedly the Gaelic League, Conradh na Gaeilge. The League, founded in Dublin in 1893, set out to preserve, promote and develop the Irish language by providing classes and lectures, publishing textbooks and newspapers, and promoting the use of the language in the educational system. It was non-sectarian and initially non-political. Under the guidance of Douglas Hyde, its first president, it succeeded in creating a new enthusiasm for the language, which crossed religious, political and social barriers. The literary and scholarly works of Hyde and contemporaries such as Eoin MacNeill, Eugene O'Growney and Canon Peter O'Leary were also responsible for awakening an interest in Irish among European linguists and academics.

With the revival of the demand for Home Rule and the advent of Sinn Féin, the League was inevitably drawn into the political arena, as the various cultural and political pressure groups overlapped and intertwined. Pádraig Pearse was co-opted onto the Executive Committee of the League in 1898, and became editor of *An Claidheamh Soluis*, the organisation's newspaper, in 1903. Many IRB activists also joined. With the formation of the Irish Volunteers in 1913 and the outbreak of war, Douglas Hyde, who was not strongly nationalist in the political sense, was replaced as president by Eoin MacNeill.

The more active involvement of the League in politics continued through 1916 and the War of Independence, since it was felt by many that the quest for cultural and political independence went hand in hand. Thomas MacDonagh, who was executed along with Pearse in 1916, was among the League's prominent members, as was Thomas Ashe who died on hunger strike in 1917.

### The Gaelic Athletic Association
The revival of interest in the language was matched by an awakening of interest in Gaelic games. The Gaelic Athletic Association, Cumann Lúthchleas Gael, was founded in 1884. It was strongly nationalist in outlook, and many of its members were also involved in political and cultural organisations. Described as one of the most successful and original mass movements of its time, it came to exert immense influence on the cultural and social life of rural Ireland.

### The Irish Parliamentary Party
The most powerful political grouping in the country, right up to 1916, was the Irish Parliamentary Party, led by Charles Stewart Parnell and later by John Redmond. Dedicated to the achievement of Home Rule by peaceful means, and skilled in parliamentary procedures, it succeeded in placing Irish issues before the British parliament and public on a scale never previously achieved. It was weakened, however, by the split between Parnellites and anti-Parnellites in the 1890s, and by the defeat of Home Rule bills in the British parliament in 1886 and 1893. Events such as the one hundredth anniversary of the 1798 rebellion, the outbreak of the Boer War, and opposition to royal visits of 1900 and 1903, all helped to galvanise various separatist groups, influenced by the Gaelic League's policy of self-reliance.

### Sinn Féin
Chief among these groups was Sinn Féin, an organisation founded by Arthur Griffith in 1905, which was later to undergo many changes of political direction. Griffith's argument was that Irish independence could be achieved by political and economic action, commencing with the refusal of Irish representatives to attend the British parliament at Westminster and the setting up of a specifically Irish civil service, court system, consular service, stock exchange and bank. Much of Griffith's early thinking was

influenced by contemporary developments in the relationship between Hungary and the Austrian Empire. His book *The Resurrection of Hungary*, published in 1904, set out many of the arguments put forward by Sinn Féin on its formation in 1905. Griffith was also influenced by the theories of the German economist Friedrich List, and he advocated the protection and development of Irish industry.

The political fortunes of Sinn Féin waned after some initial electoral successes, but its doctrine of self-reliance in politics, economics and culture had a much wider influence. After the 1916 Rising, sometimes referred to incorrectly as the 'Sinn Féin Rebellion', the party came to stand for a policy of militant resistance to British rule. It won a number of by-elections in 1917, before winning a sweeping victory in the General Election of 1918. This was followed by the setting up of an Irish parliament, Dáil Éireann, and an even more comprehensive victory at the polls in 1921.

## ARMS AND ARMIES

*Photo 1. UVF 1st Battalion, North Down Regiment, on parade, 1912.*

### The Ulster Volunteer Force

While the various literary, cultural and political separatists were interacting and indeed coalescing in such people as Pádraig Pearse and Thomas MacDonagh, Home Rule appeared on the political agenda once again. In 1912 a bill put forward by the ruling Liberal Party, and supported by the Irish Parliamentary Party, was passed by the House of Commons. Because of parliamentary reform initiated the previous year, the House of Lords could not block the bill beyond 1914. As it became apparent that the bill would not be defeated in parliament, unionists became increasingly

determined to block its implementation by whatever means possible. The
Conservative party under the leadership of Andrew Bonar Law supported
this approach, with Bonar Law declaring that 'there are things stronger than
parliamentary majorities'. On 28 September the Solemn League and
Covenant was launched 'to defeat the present conspiracy to set up a Home
Rule parliament in Ireland'. Signatories pledged that if such a parliament
were to be set up, they would refuse to recognise its authority. The
covenant, signed by over two hundred thousand people, was followed by
the launching of the Ulster Volunteer Force (UVF), which drilled and
trained openly and commenced to import arms. The most dramatic
landing of arms took place on 24 April 1914, when thirty-five thousand
rifles were landed at the Ulster ports of Larne, Bangor and Donaghadee.

### The Irish Volunteers

The UVF was an extremely significant innovation on the
Irish political scene. Its activities were noted and almost
immediately copied by Irish nationalists, while attempts to
curb it led to an incident in 1914 known as the 'Curragh
Mutiny', when senior British officers refused to move against
it. The first nationalist group to follow the precedent set by
the UVF was the Midland Volunteer Force, formed in
Athlone in September 1913. This was soon followed by the
formation of the Irish Volunteers and the Irish Citizen Army,
with the Irish Volunteers absorbing the Midland Volunteers.
The example of the unionists was not lost on the
nationalists. As Pádraig Pearse put it: 'Personally, I think the
Orangeman with a rifle a much less ridiculous figure than
the Nationalist without a rifle.' The nationalists, accordingly,
followed the UVF example and began to arm.

*Photo 2. Handbill
announcing the
formation of the
Irish Volunteers on
25 November 1913.*

The Irish Volunteers were formed at a meeting in the Rotunda, Dublin,
on 25 November 1913. Many of the key positions were filled by members
of the IRB and the republican boy scout movement, Na Fianna. The Irish
Parliamentary Party initially opposed but later attempted to take control of
the movement, and John Redmond succeeded in placing twenty-five of his

*Photo 3. Springlawn
Volunteers,
Co Galway, 1914.
Battalions of Irish
Volunteers sprang up
throughout the
country following the
formation of the
movement in
November 1913.*

nominees on the Provisional Committee. The Volunteers spread rapidly, despite the action of the government in prohibiting the importation of arms. The successful landing of major consignments of rifles at Howth in County Dublin and Kilcoole in County Wicklow in July and August 1914 was a major practical and propaganda boost for the movement.

*Photo 4. Irish
Volunteers returning
from Howth,
Co Dublin, with
Mauser rifles, July
1914. The guns
were purchased in
Hamburg and
dispatched to
Ireland on the
Asgard, a yacht
owned by Erskine
Childers, one of the
organisers of the
operation.*

The outbreak of World War I brought out into the open all the internal strains and tensions that until then had remained beneath the surface. As a body that had been founded openly and drilled openly, the Volunteers had been infiltrated by almost every pressure group in the country. John Redmond offered the Volunteers' services to Britain to help with the war effort, much to the anger of the IRB and Sinn Féin, who believed that Irish blood should only be shed in Ireland. Roger Casement, a committed nationalist involved in arming the Irish Volunteers, demanded that 'if this be a war for the small nationalities, as its planners assert, then let it begin, for one small nationality, at home'. The inevitable split that followed led to the formation of two distinct bodies, the National Volunteers, who joined the British Army in large numbers, and the

*Photo 5. Two generations of revolutionaries: Roger Casement and John Devoy in America, 1914.*

Irish Volunteers. The latter group, officially under the chairmanship of Eoin MacNeill, came increasingly under the control and influence of the IRB, who with the backing of Clan na Gael in America, made contact with Germany, commenced the importation of arms and began to prepare for armed rebellion.

## The Irish Citizen Army

Not all the agitation and plotting was purely political in nature. In Dublin the Irish Citizen Army, under James Connolly, was also planning for revolution. The origins of the Citizen Army may be traced to the deplorable living conditions of the urban working classes in the early years of the twentieth century. Wages were low, especially for unskilled labour, and housing in Belfast and Dublin was among the worst 'in Europe. In

*Photo 6. Boys 'playing soldiers' in the vicinity of Liberty Hall, Dublin, 1914. The diet, clothing and general living conditions of the urban poor were among the worst in Europe.*

*Photo 7. The arrest of
trade union leader Jim
Larkin during the 1913
lock-out in Dublin.
Having been prohibited
from addressing a public
meeting, he had
successfully disguised
himself in order to
deliver his speech.*

*Photo 8. Trade union
handbill published by
the Amalgamated
Society of Tailors. Firms
that refused to employ
unionised labour were
fiercely opposed by the
growing labour
movement.*

*Photo 9. A riot in
O'Connell Street,
Dublin, 1913. Police
violence against the
strikers led to the
formation of the Irish
Citizen Army, as a
workers' defence
association.*

*Photo 10. Food voucher,
issued during the 1913
lock-out. Support from
British trade unions for
their Dublin colleagues
was initially substantial,
but dwindled as the
strike wore on.*

7.

8.

# Workers!
## SUPPORT YOUR FELLOW-WORKERS.
# Don't Wear Clothes
## MADE BY
# SCAB LABOUR

In Henry Street and Mary Street the following Firms
do not employ any Trade Union Tailors:—
The Donegal Tweed Co., Dundon & Co., James
O'Dwyer, Karmel, Morris, Richardson, Bailey, Webb &
Co., Maple & Co., J. J. Kenny, Lyons & Co., and The
Eagle Tailoring Co.

The Trade Union Firms are:—
Arnott & Co., The Henry Street Warehouse Co.,
Todd Burns & Co., and Dallas.

**Help the Tailors to Stamp Out
the Sweating System.**

Before Leaving Orders for Clothes send for
Fair List to the Secretary, Tailors' Society,
Trades' Hall.

Published by the Amalgamated Society of Tailors and Printed by Trades' Union
Labour in Dublin on Irish Paper.

9.

BRITISH TRADES UNION CONGRESS &
DUBLIN TRADES COUNCIL.

BRITISH TRADE UNION FUND.

Give Bearer Parcel Bread, &c.

Apply—South Wall. From 12 noon to 6 p.m.
SECOND ISSUE.
J. A. SEDDON,
T. MacPARTLIN.

O'KEEFFE, Trade Union Printer, 3 Halston St., Dublin.

10. BRITISH TRADES UNION CONGRESS &
DUBLIN TRADES COUNCIL.

BRITISH TRADE UNION FUND.

Give Bearer Parcel Bread, &c.

Apply—South Wall. From 12 noon to 6
p.m. Saturday, 27th Sept., 1913.
J. A. SEDDON,
T. MacPARTLIN.

O'KEEFFE, Trade Union Printer, 3 Halston St., Dublin.

Photo 11. Irish Citizen
Army members on the
roof of Liberty Hall,
Dublin, headquarters
of the Transport
Union.

Photo 12. Irish Citizen
Army mobilisation
order, May 1915. The
procuring of arms and
equipment posed
considerable difficulties,
and uniforms were
purchased piecemeal by
the members themselves.

1911 the death rate in Dublin was put at 27.6 per 1000, the highest in
Europe (the next highest being Moscow).

In August 1913 the simmering unrest in Dublin came to a head in a
number of strikes for better wages and working conditions, which in turn
led to a lock-out. The workers, with their leader Jim Larkin, faced the
Employers' Federation led by William Martin Murphy, in a bitter struggle
which culminated in considerable street violence. Rallies by the increasingly
desperate workers were met by indiscriminate baton charges from the
police. Several deaths resulted, many were injured and numerous arrests
were made. The strikers were sustained for a time by food ships and aid
from England, but as solidarity and support dwindled they were gradually
forced back to work, largely on the employers' terms. The Citizen Army
was formed in November 1913, at the height of the strike, as a workers'

defence association. Roused by the oratory of Larkin, controlled by James Connolly, and drilled by Captain J R White at Croydon Park (the Transport Union grounds at Fairview), the organisation survived the collapse of the strike and gradually began to arm itself. Despite considerable initial friction and suspicion between the Citizen Army and the larger Volunteer movement, the two bodies moved closer together after the outbreak of World War I, and fought side by side in 1916. James Connolly and his second-in-command, Michael Mallin, were among those executed after the Rising.

## THE OUTBREAK OF WORLD WAR I

*Photo 13. Irish troops in the trenches during World War I. Irishmen joined the British Army in great numbers, in answer to John Redmond's call and to Allied claims that they were fighting for the freedom of small nations.*

*Pl 1. (Facing page) Appointment of Thomas J Clarke as an adjutant in the Irish Volunteers, New York, 1906. The Irish Volunteers in question here were associated with Clan na Gael, the American wing of the IRB, and should not be confused with the movement formed later in Dublin to support Home Rule.*

On 28 June 1914 Archduke Franz Ferdinand of Austria was assassinated, triggering off one of the bloodiest wars of all time. Most of Europe and the colonies of European countries in Africa and Asia became involved, as did the Turkish Empire and, later, the USA. Total casualties, military and civilian, have been estimated at fifteen million dead and more than twice that number wounded. Huge numbers of Irishmen, both nationalists and unionists, joined the British Army, encouraged by a massive recruiting drive, by the British claim that they were fighting for the freedom of small nations, and by John Redmond's declaration that the war was about 'right, freedom and religion'. They suffered enormous casualties on the various fronts, especially the Battle of the Somme and the attack on Gallipoli, as

*cont. p 33*

# IRISH VOLUNTEERS

To *Thomas J Clarke*

GREETING :

Reposing special trust and confidence as well in your patriotism, conduct and loyalty, as in your integrity and readiness to do good and faithful service, have appointed and constituted and by these presents do appoint and constitute you the said *Thomas J Clarke Regimental Adjutant in the 2nd Infantry* with rank from *January 1st 1906*

You are therefore to observe and follow such orders and directions as you shall from time to time receive from the Headquarters of the Irish Volunteers or any of your superior officers, according to the Military Code and Regulations of the Irish Volunteers, and hold the same office in the manner specified therein.

In pursuance of the trust imposed on you and for so doing this shall be your COMMISSION.

IN TESTIMONY WHEREOF, we have caused the Seal for Commissions to be hereunto affixed.

Witness : JOHN P. SCANLON, Assistant Adjutant-General, Irish Volunteers, at New York, N. Y., *January 6th 1906*

*John P Scanlon*
Assistant Adjutant-General.

*M. F. O'Rourke*
Aide de Camp

*Pl 2. Gaelic League poster by Sadhbh Trinnseach, c. 1910–15. The League's gospel of independence and self-reliance had a powerful influence on other nationalist bodies. Pádraig Pearse believed that it would be 'recognised in history as the most revolutionary influence that has ever come into Ireland'.*

*Pl 3. Ulster's Solemn League and Covenant, 28 September 1912. The covenant was signed, in the words of Sir Edward Carson, 'by soldiers in uniform, policemen in uniform and men in the pay of the government and they dared not touch one of them'.*

# Ulster's
## Solemn League and Covenant.

**B**eing convinced in our consciences that Home Rule would be disastrous to the material well-being of Ulster as well as of the whole of Ireland, subversive of our civil and religious freedom, destructive of our citizenship and perilous to the unity of the Empire, we, whose names are underwritten, men of Ulster, loyal subjects of His Gracious Majesty King George V., humbly relying on the God whom our fathers in days of stress and trial confidently trusted, do hereby pledge ourselves in solemn Covenant throughout this our time of threatened calamity to stand by one another in defending for ourselves and our children our cherished position of equal citizenship in the United Kingdom and in using all means which may be found necessary to defeat the present conspiracy to set up a Home Rule Parliament in Ireland. ¶ And in the event of such a Parliament being forced upon us we further solemnly and mutually pledge ourselves to refuse to recognise its authority. ¶ In sure confidence that God will defend the right we hereto subscribe our names. ¶ And further, we individually declare that we have not already signed this Covenant.

The above was signed by me at_____
"Ulster Day." Saturday, 28th September, 1912.

## God Save the King.

*Pl 4. UVF banner,
2nd Battalion, West
Down Regiment.*

*Pl 5. Irish Volunteers'
membership card,
1913. Members were
encouraged 'to drill, to
learn the use of arms, to
acquire the habit of
concerted and
disciplined action, to
form a citizen army
from a population now
at the mercy of almost
any organised
aggression', an obvious
reference to the Ulster
unionists and their
British supporters.*

**OBJECTS OF THE IRISH
VOLUNTEERS.**

1. To secure and maintain the
   rights and liberties common
   to the people of Ireland.

2. To train, discipline, and
   equip for this purpose an
   Irish Volunteer Force.

3. To unite, in the service of
   Ireland, Irishmen of every
   creed, and of every party
   and class.

Oglaiġ na héireann
(The Irish Volunteers)

No. 02667

**Membership
Card**

*Pl 6. Labour handbill, 'An diabhal in uachtar in Áth Cliath' (The devil supreme in Dublin). The conflict between employers and workers, which was waged with great ferocity, was said to have been 'chiefly remarkable for the relentless tenacity shown by both sides'.*

*Pl 7. Uniforms of the Irish Citizen Army, from a watercolour by Eileen Johnson. The 'Red Hand' motif (visible on the cap badge), more commonly associated with Ulster, was also the symbol of the Irish Transport and General Workers' Union (ITGWU).*

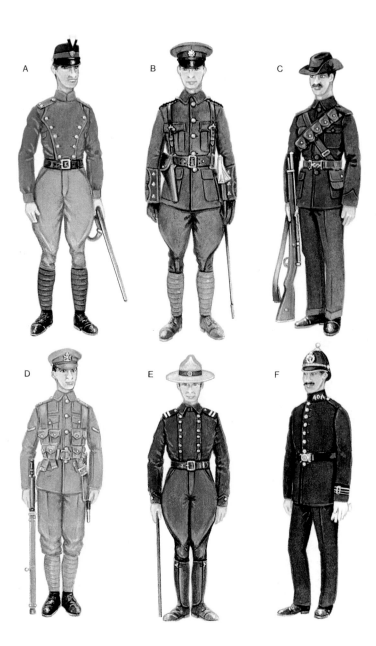

*Pl 8. Uniforms:
a) Private, Irish
National Guard, 1911
(a small nationalist
organisation)
b) Captain, Irish
Volunteers, 1915
c) Private, Irish
Citizen Army, 1914
d) Lance-corporal,
Sherwood Foresters,
British Army, 1916
e) Commandant,
Fianna Éireann, 1915
f) Constable, Dublin
Metropolitan Police,
1916*

*(From a watercolour by
Glenn Thompson.)*

*Pl 9. (Facing page) The 'Signatories Page' from Leabhar na hAiséirighe (The Book of the Resurrection) by Art O'Murnaghan. Consisting of twenty-six pages and intended as a memorial to those who had died in the fight for independence, the work was commissioned in 1922 and finally completed in 1951. O'Murnaghan, painter, actor, stage designer and teacher, died in 1954.*

*Pl 10. The Starry Plough, flag of the Irish Citizen Army. The suggestion that the Citizen Army should have its own flag apparently came from the trade union leader Jim Larkin. During Easter week it was hoisted over the Imperial Hotel in O'Connell Street on the orders of James Connolly, perhaps as a gesture, since the hotel was owned by William Martin Murphy, leader of the Employers' Federation.*

*Pl 11. The 'Irish Republic' flag that was flown over the GPO during Easter week, 1916. The flag survived the bombardment and burning of the building, and it was taken away by British troops after the surrender of the insurgents. It was presented by the British government to the Irish government in 1966.*

*Pl 12. Execution scene,
Kilmainham Jail, May
1916. Unsigned. The
long-drawn-out nature
of the executions, and
particularly that of the
wounded James
Connolly, had a
dramatic and
immediate effect on
public opinion, which
was manifested in a
major swing towards
Sinn Féin in 1917/18.*

*Pls 13–19. Charcoal
and pastel drawings of
executed 1916 leaders
by Seán O'Sullivan,
RHA.*

13. *Pádraig Pearse (b. Dublin 1879)
Poet, writer, educationalist, lawyer and
revolutionary, he was commander-in-chief
during Easter week. He was proclaimed president
of the provisional government and he read and
signed the Proclamation of Independence. He
surrendered to General Lowe on 29 April and
was executed on 3 May. His younger brother
William was executed the following day.*

14. *Thomas Clarke (b. Isle of Wight 1857)
Veteran Fenian leader and one of the chief
planners of the Rising. He joined Clan na
Gael in the United States, was arrested in
England and spent fifteen years in prison. He
returned to Ireland in 1907 and helped to
reorganise the IRB. The first to sign the
Proclamation and the oldest of the signatories,
he was executed on 3 May.*

15. *Thomas MacDonagh (b. Cloughjordan,
Co Tipperary, 1878)
Teacher, poet, Gaelic League member and
director of training in the Irish Volunteers. A
member of the IRB's Military Council, he was
one of the principal organisers of the insurrection.
He commanded the 2nd Battalion, Dublin
Brigade, during 1916, and was executed, with
Connolly and Clarke, on 3 May.*

16. *Joseph Plunkett (b. Dublin 1887)
Poet, writer and editor, he was one of the
founders of the Irish Volunteers. He visited
America and Germany in 1915 to seek
support and arms for the Rising. He married
Grace Gifford on 3 May in Kilmainham Jail
and was executed the following day.*

17. *Seán MacDiarmada (b. Kiltyclogher,
Co Leitrim, 1884)
Joined the IRB in 1906 and later became
treasurer of its Supreme Council. He organised
the IRB publication* Irish Freedom *and he was
also involved in organising the Irish Volunteers.
He was a member of the Gaelic League, Sinn
Féin and the Gaelic Athletic Association.
Although crippled by polio he fought in the GPO
in 1916 and was executed on 12 May.*

18. *Eamonn Ceannt (b. Glenamaddy,
Co Galway, 1881)
A prominent member of the Gaelic League
and a fine musician, he was elected onto the
Provisional Committee of the Irish Volunteers
in 1913. A member of the Military Council of
the IRB, he commanded the 4th Battalion of
the Volunteers in 1916 and was executed on
8 May.*

19. *James Connolly (b. Edinburgh 1868)
Socialist thinker and labour activist, he founded*
The Workers' Republic, *the first Irish socialist
newspaper, in 1898. He spent several years in the
United States as a union organiser before
returning to Ireland in 1910. With James Larkin
he led the workers in the 1913 Lock-out and was
one of the founders of the Irish Citizen Army. He
was commandant-general, Dublin district,
during the Rising, and was executed on 12 May.*

*Pl 20. Bone Celtic
cross, Frongoch
Internment Camp,
Wales, 1916–17.
Frongoch had initially
housed German
prisoners of war, but
these were moved out to
make way for the Irish
after 1916.*

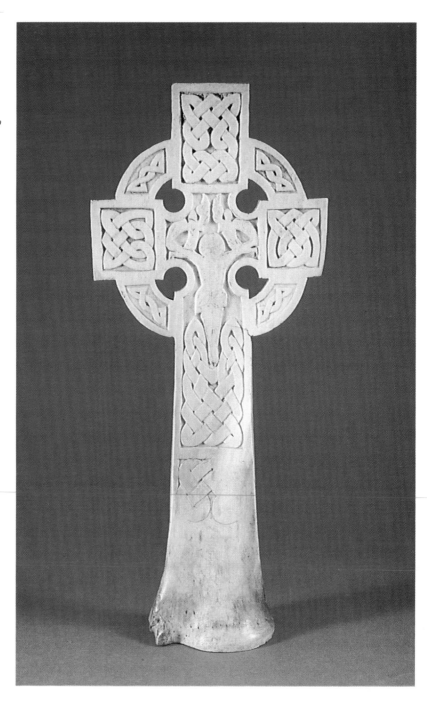

XMAS '17

DES. 4501

Pl 21. Prisoners'
Christmas card, 1917.
The places named are
prisons where Sinn
Féin activists and
sympathisers were held
after 1916.

Sinn Fein

DE VALERA BRANCH,

COMP. ED. DE VALERA.

BAILIEBORO.

August- 1917.

Pl 22. Flag of the
Bailieboro, Co Cavan,
branch of Sinn Féin,
1917. The branch was
named after Éamon de
Valera, the senior
surviving Volunteer
commandant from
1916. De Valera was
imprisoned in English
jails in Dartmoor,
Maidstone, Lewes and
Pentonville, before
being released in June
1917, and he was to
become a major figure
in Irish politics for over
half a century.

*Pl 23. Postcard/cartoon
commemorating 1916.
Unsigned.*

*Pl 24. National Defence Fund, Ballyhaunis, Co Mayo, 1918. The decision of the British government to extend conscription to Ireland in April 1918 met with fierce opposition from Irish nationalists. An anti-conscription pledge was drawn up and a Defence Fund organised. The ferocity of the opposition forced the authorities to postpone implementation of the measure.*

*Pl 25. Irish Victory Fund, New York, 1919. Irish-Americans contributed huge sums of money to the republican cause, especially during the period 1919–21. The Victory Fund was set up following an Irish Race Convention held in Philadelphia in February 1919, and it raised a considerable sum of money for use in Ireland.*

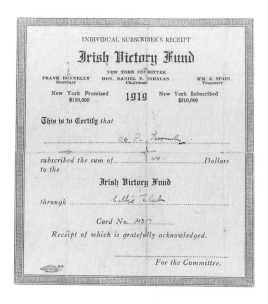

*Pl 26. Republican Bond, twenty-five dollars, 1920. In order to raise funds for the new government departments, a Dáil Loan was organised in 1919, under the control of Michael Collins. In 1920 an External Loan was floated in the USA by Éamon de Valera, money was raised through Irish-American organisations, and over five million dollars was collected for use in Ireland.*

*Pl 27. Handkerchief, from Ballykinlar Internment Camp, Co Down, signed 'O. Nevin. 1921'. Prison craftwork was produced from whatever material happened to be available — wood, bone, textile, paper or, less commonly, metal.*

*Pl 28. Medals relating to the period 1916 to 1921. Viewed from left to right:*
*1) awarded to 1916 participants;*
*2) issued to survivors on 50th anniversary, 1966;*
*3) awarded to those who took part in the War of Independence;*
*4) issued to survivors on the 50th anniversary of the Truce, 1971.*

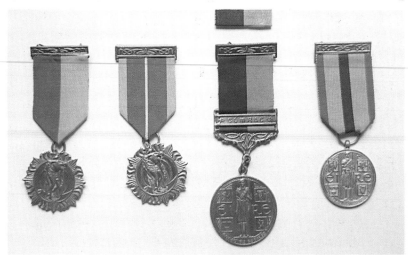

*cont. from p 16*

the war that was to be 'over by Christmas' became bogged down in the trenches.

Upon the outbreak of the war the Supreme Council of the IRB actively set about planning a rebellion. Contact was made with Germany by Roger Casement and Joseph Plunkett, and the IRB tightened its control over the Irish Volunteers. A Military Committee that had been set up to plan the rebellion was replaced by a Military Council in 1915, comprising Pádraig Pearse, Eamonn Ceannt, Joseph Plunkett, Seán Mac Diarmada and Thomas Clarke. Casement's attempts to form an Irish Brigade among Irish prisoners in Germany were largely unsuccessful, but a promise of German arms was received and there was growing co-operation between the Military Council and the Citizen Army. Some of James Connolly's socialist contemporaries were uneasy at the thought of alliance with conservative nationalists. His own reading of the situation, however, was characteristically blunt: 'We believe in constitutional action in normal times; we believe in revolutionary action in exceptional times. These are exceptional times.' It was a rather confused and confusing period, with the IRB keeping the Irish Volunteers' chairman Eoin MacNeill 'in the dark' regarding their plans. Internally, the Supreme Council was not always privy to the plans of the Military Council. John Devoy and Clan na Gael (the American wing of the IRB) were negotiating with Germany, often without the knowledge of Roger Casement, who was about the same business.

## THE RISING AND ITS AFTERMATH

By January 1916 the Supreme Council of the IRB had decided upon 23 April as the date for the commencement of the rebellion. This was later changed to 24 April, and plans were made to take delivery of arms and munitions from Germany. When Eoin MacNeill discovered at the last moment that a rebellion was being planned, he countermanded the mobilisation orders, changed his mind when told that the German arms were on their way, and changed it again when he heard of their capture. Meanwhile the Military Council — by this time it included James Connolly, leader of the Irish Citizen Army — decided to take action on Easter Monday, 24 April.

*Photo 14. Irish
Volunteers'
mobilisation order, 23
April 1916. The
issuing and
countermanding of
mobilisation orders
caused much confusion
and ensured the failure
of the insurrection.*

*Photo 15. Cumann na
mBan member in
uniform, 1916.
Although the
organisation was
founded as an auxiliary
to the Irish Volunteers,
it was a separate body
with its own
constitution and
executive.*

*Photo 16. (Facing
page) The
Proclamation of
Independence, 1916.
The seven signatories
were among those
executed after the
surrender.*

*Photo 17. (Facing
page) Countess
Markievicz in uniform,
c. 1915. One of the
most colourful figures
of the period, she was
associated with almost
every nationalist
organisation. She
fought in the 1916
Rising, spent time in
prison, became
Minister for Labour in
the first Dáil and again
in 1921. She died in
1927.*

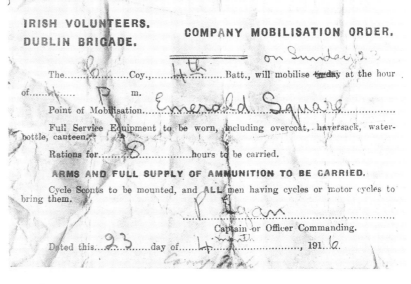

Following MacNeill's counter-manding order, however, and the loss of the German ammunition ship, the *Aud*, any chance of a successful uprising disappeared. The conflicting instructions furthermore meant that there was little military activity outside Dublin. On the morning of 24 April a twelve-hundred-strong force of Volunteer and Citizen Army members, together with a contingent from Cumann na mBan, the republican women's organisation, took over the centre of the city. The Proclamation of Independence was read from the General Post Office (GPO) and an Irish Republic declared, with

16.

## POBLACHT NA H EIREANN.
### THE PROVISIONAL GOVERNMENT
OF THE
# IRISH REPUBLIC
## TO THE PEOPLE OF IRELAND.

IRISHMEN AND IRISHWOMEN : In the name of God and of the dead generations from which she receives her old tradition of nationhood, Ireland, through us, summons her children to her flag and strikes for her freedom.

Having organised and trained her manhood through her secret revolutionary organisation, the Irish Republican Brotherhood, and through her open military organisations, the Irish Volunteers and the Irish Citizen Army, having patiently perfected her discipline, having resolutely waited for the right moment to reveal itself, she now seizes that moment, and, supported by her exiled children in America and by gallant allies in Europe, but relying in the first on her own strength, she strikes in full confidence of victory.

We declare the right of the people of Ireland to the ownership of Ireland, and to the unfettered control of Irish destinies, to be sovereign and indefeasible. The long usurpation of that right by a foreign people and government has not extinguished the right, nor can it ever be extinguished except by the destruction of the Irish people. In every generation the Irish people have asserted their right to national freedom and sovereignty ; six times during the past three hundred years they have asserted it in arms. Standing on that fundamental right and again asserting it in arms in the face of the world, we hereby proclaim the Irish Republic as a Sovereign Independent State, and we pledge our lives and the lives of our comrades-in-arms to the cause of its freedom, of its welfare, and of its exaltation among the nations.

The Irish Republic is entitled to, and hereby claims, the allegiance of every Irishman and Irishwoman. The Republic guarantees religious and civil liberty, equal rights and equal opportunities to all its citizens, and declares its resolve to pursue the happiness and prosperity of the whole nation and of all its parts, cherishing all the children of the nation equally, and oblivious of the differences carefully fostered by an alien government, which have divided a minority from the majority in the past.

Until our arms have brought the opportune moment for the establishment of a permanent National Government, representative of the whole people of Ireland and elected by the suffrages of all her men and women, the Provisional Government, hereby constituted, will administer the civil and military affairs of the Republic in trust for the people.

We place the cause of the Irish Republic under the protection of the Most High God, Whose blessing we invoke upon our arms, and we pray that no one who serves that cause will dishonour it by cowardice, inhumanity, or rapine. In this supreme hour the Irish nation must, by its valour and discipline and by the readiness of its children to sacrifice themselves for the common good, prove itself worthy of the august destiny to which it is called.

Signed on Behalf of the Provisional Government,

THOMAS J. CLARKE,
SEAN Mac DIARMADA,   THOMAS MacDONAGH,
P. H. PEARSE,   EAMONN CEANNT,
JAMES CONNOLLY.   JOSEPH PLUNKETT.

17.

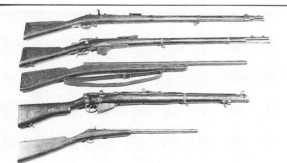

*Photo 18. Rifles of the Rising. The Volunteers were armed with a motley collection of Mausers, Lee Enfields, Winchesters, Italian and other rifles. The 'firearm' in the centre is a wooden training gun.*

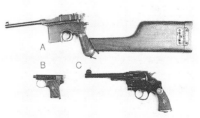

*Photo 19. Handguns of the Rising: a) Mauser automatic owned by Countess Markievicz, b) Webley and Scott semi-automatic owned by Con Colbert, c) Smith and Wesson revolver owned by Captain de Courcy Wheeler.*

Pádraig Pearse as president of the provisional government. The Proclamation was signed by Pearse and six others, Thomas Clarke, Seán Mac Diarmada, James Connolly, Thomas MacDonagh, Eamonn Ceannt and Joseph Plunkett. Garrisons were established at the Four Courts, Bolands Mills, Jacobs Factory, the South Dublin Union, the College of Surgeons and several other strategic points. The City Hall was also captured.

The insurgent force was augmented on the first day by small groups which managed to get through before the British military cordon was in place, including a unit of the Hibernian Rifles, a small armed group associated with a wing of the Ancient Order of Hibernians. There followed five days of fierce fighting as British forces, aided by artillery from Athlone, reinforcements from the Curragh, County Kildare, and a gunboat on the river Liffey, slowly encircled and isolated the various garrisons. Some of the heaviest fighting took place around Mount Street Bridge, as British reinforcements moving in from Dún Laoghaire encountered fierce opposition. Heavy hand-to-hand fighting also took place around the Four Courts and other strategic points. The failure of the insurgents to capture Trinity College or Dublin Castle allowed the British to drive a wedge between posts north and south of the river and bring artillery to bear on the GPO. By Thursday afternoon the British forces had been greatly strengthened and they succeeded in isolating the GPO from other insurgent positions. The following night its garrison was forced to evacuate the building. The insurgents retreated into Moore Street, from where they attempted to tunnel their way to a stronger position, carrying the wounded Connolly in a sheet, as his stretcher would not fit through the tunnel openings. The situation was hopeless, however, as they were now surrounded on all sides, and O'Rahilly, one of their bravest commanders, lay dead in Moore Street. Finally, on Saturday 29 April, with the GPO in flames and the centre of the city in ruins, Pearse gave the order to surrender.

Much has been said and written regarding the insurrection — its timing, its significance and its influence on subsequent political developments. Contemporaries and historians have agreed on one point however, the heroism and selflessness of those who willingly risked all for what, in the

20.

21.

22.

24.

23.

circumstances, was a doomed undertaking. Even Herbert Asquith, the British Prime Minister, accepted in the House of Commons that 'they conducted themselves with great humanity, which contrasted very much to their advantage with some of the so-called civilised enemies with which we are fighting in Europe'. The initial media reaction to the Rising, however, was outright condemnation. The immediate reaction of the general public, in so far as it can be ascertained, was one of bewilderment, confusion and some hostility. All this was to change rapidly as events unfolded in the following days.

*Photo 25. Group of British officers with the 'Irish Republic' flag that was taken from the GPO after the surrender of the insurgents in Easter week 1916.*

General Maxwell, who arrived in Dublin to take control of the British forces on 28 April, promptly court-martialled and executed the principal leaders of the Rising. The executions began on 3 May when Pádraig Pearse, Thomas MacDonagh and Thomas Clarke were shot by firing squad in Kilmainham Jail. Over the next eight days a further twelve executions were carried out, despite growing protests in Ireland, Britain and America. Those executed included the seven signatories of the Proclamation, together with Con Colbert, Seán Heuston, Michael Mallin, Michael O'Hanrahan, William Pearse, John MacBride, Edward Daly and, in Cork, Thomas Kent. Over ninety others were sentenced to death, but had their sentences commuted. Roger Casement, who had travelled from Germany at the same

*Photo 26. Prisoners on
the quays, Dublin, en
route to internment in
Britain, May 1916.*

*Photo 27. Prisoners
from Enniscorthy, Co
Wexford, arriving at
Kilmainham Jail, May
1916.*

time as the *Aud*, was captured and hanged for treason on
3 August. Of those arrested after the Rising, most were
interned in British prisons, such as Knutsford, Lewes,
Glasgow, Stafford, Wakefield, Wandsworth and Perth.
Later, about eighteen hundred were transferred to an
internment camp at Frongoch in Wales. Here they elected
their own leaders, studied the Irish language and history,
and generally maintained their own organisation. The

majority of these were released in August, the remainder in December. The
convicted prisoners were released in June 1917 and were welcomed home
as heroes.

*Photo 28. John Dillon,
leader of the Irish
Parliamentary Party,
addressing an anti-
conscription meeting at
Ballaghaderreen, Co
Roscommon, 1918.*

The dramatic swing in public opinion that followed the execution of the 1916 leaders manifested itself in the by-elections of 1917, and was given further impetus by the threat of conscription. The huge losses sustained by the British Army on the Western Front prompted the British government to extend conscription to Ireland in April 1918. The proposal met with fierce opposition, however, and brought together Sinn Féin, the Irish Parliamentary Party, the Labour movement and church leaders in a rare show of unity. An anti-conscription pledge was drawn up and was signed by hundreds of thousands. The British reintroduced internment and imprisoned most of the Sinn Féin leadership, in England. The Volunteers prepared to resist conscription by arms, but the signing of the Armistice on 11 November brought the crisis to an end.

Following the General Election of December 1918 the Sinn Féin representatives refused to attend Westminster and instead established an Irish parliament, Dáil Éireann, on 21 January 1919. The Dáil immediately elected a president and cabinet and set about the business of government. In April it decreed the issue of Republican Bonds to finance its work. Departments were organised and an unsuccessful attempt was made to gain international recognition for Ireland at the Paris Peace Conference. In June the Dáil decreed the setting up of national arbitration courts and the establishment of a consular service. It also began to become more involved in social and economic issues, allocating funds for forestation and fisheries

*Photo 29. Members of the first Dáil, January 1919. Following its 1918 election success, Sinn Féin called a meeting at the Mansion House, Dublin, which non-republicans boycotted. Those who attended — many Sinn Féin members were in jail — set up Dáil Éireann, the Irish parliament.*

and setting up a Land Bank. As the military conflict escalated, however, it came under steadily increasing pressure from the British authorities, and was finally banned on 10 September.

## THE WAR OF INDEPENDENCE 1919–21

During 1917 and 1918 the Volunteers, spear-headed by 1916 survivors and released internees, began to rearm. At first there was no unified policy on how arms were to be procured. What was later to develop into large-scale guerilla warfare initially took the form of raids for arms. The first major raid was at Soloheadbeg, County Tipperary, in January 1919, and as the year wore on the attacks, especially on Royal Irish Constabulary (RIC) barracks, intensified. The RIC were gradually driven back to the larger towns and the regular British Army was increasingly brought into use. By the end of the year there were over forty thousand troops in the country.

The fighting intensified in 1920 as raids, reprisals, curfews and large-scale military sweeps became commonplace. A new force which became known as the Black and Tans was recruited in Britain for service in Ireland, as the regular army began to lose the battle for control of the countryside. Their name came from their improvised uniform, often of police tunic and khaki trousers. They gained an unenviable reputation for violence, arson and murder. Given the task of making Ireland 'an appropriate hell for those whose trade is agitation', they succeeded in making it a hell for the population in general. A second force, recruited largely from ex-army officers, and known as the Auxiliaries, was also sent as a back-up to the increasingly demoralised RIC. The Volunteers, who now generally referred to themselves as the Irish Republican Army (IRA), perfected a type of guerilla warfare based upon flying columns and active service units, which was extremely difficult to combat.

Meanwhile events such as the hanging of Kevin Barry, an eighteen-year-old Volunteer, and the murder by police officers of Tomás MacCurtain, Mayor of Cork, focused world attention on the Irish situation, as did hunger strikes by republicans seeking prisoner-of-war status. The death on hunger strike of Thomas Ashe in 1917 had been followed by some

*Photo 30. Bronze bust of Seán Treacy, by Kathleen Parbury. One of the most fearless of the post-1916 generation of guerilla fighters, Treacy was involved in the Soloheadbeg ambush, regarded as the first armed incident of the War of Independence. He was shot dead during a gun battle in Dublin on 14 October 1920.*

*cont. p 44*

*Photo 31. British Army cordon outside the National Museum, Kildare Street, Dublin, 1920.*

*Photo 32. British soldier searching cyclist on Dublin street, 1920. Street searches, military dragnets and curfews became increasingly common as the warfare intensified.*

31.

33.

*Photo 33. British troops searching motorcar, Dublin, 1920.*

*Photo 34. Group of Black and Tans on Union Quay, Cork, 1920.*

34.

35.

36.

37.

38.

Photo 35. Auxiliaries
on patrol, 1921.
Recruited largely from
among British officers
who had fought in the
1914–18 war, they
were officially deemed
to be police and were
not under the control of
the regular army.

Photo 36. The Lord
Lieutenant, Field
Marshal French,
reviewing RIC
constables in the police
depot, Phoenix Park,
1921.

Photo 38. Republican
hunger-striker being
taken from Mountjoy
Jail to the Mater
Hospital, 1920.

Photo 37. IRA Volunteers, West
Mayo Brigade, 1921. The highly
mobile columns and guerilla tactics
used by the IRA enabled them to
tie down the numerically superior
and better armed British forces.

Photo 39. Women protesting outside Mountjoy Jail, Dublin,
during a hunger-strike by republican prisoners, 1920.

*cont. from p 41*

*Photo 40. Death mask
of Terence MacSwiney
by Albert Power, RHA.
MacSwiney's hunger-
strike and death gained
international attention
and sympathy for the
republican cause.*

*Photo 41. British
troops on the roof of the
Four Courts, Dublin,
1921.*

concessions, but the issue re-emerged in 1920 as the jails and camps filled up with internees. In Mountjoy prison in Dublin, sixty inmates went on hunger strike in April 1920, forcing the authorities to introduce new regulations for the treatment of prisoners. Irish prisoners in Wormwood Scrubs prison in England took similar action and were eventually released. The event which more than any other gained international attention, however, was the death in October 1920 of Terence MacSwiney in Brixton Prison, after seventy-four days on hunger strike. MacSwiney was MacCurtain's successor as Lord Mayor of Cork, IRA brigade commander and TD for Mid Cork in the Dáil. His belief that 'it is not those who can inflict the most, but those who can endure the most who will conquer' was certainly prophetic. His death and the death of two prisoners in Cork Jail gained huge sympathy for Sinn Féin.

As the armed conflict intensified, the existing prisons were unable to cope with the huge flood of prisoners. A number of internment camps were set up, such as those at Spike Island in County Cork and Ballykinlar in

*Photo 42. James Daly, 1st Battalion, Connaught Rangers, executed 2 July 1920. In June 1920, three hundred and fifty members of the regiment, stationed in the Punjab, India, mutinied in protest against British atrocities in Ireland. Sixty-two were court-martialled and Daly was executed.*

*Photo 43. The 'Sack of Balbriggan', Dublin, 20 September 1920. A resident removes belongings salvaged after the Black and Tans burned twenty-five houses in the village as a reprisal for the shooting of one of their members in the vicinity.*

*Photo 44. The aftermath of a Black and Tan attack on Templemore, Co Tipperary, August 1920.*

*Photo 45. The burning of the Custom House, 25 May 1921. The building housed several government departments, and its destruction by the IRA was a major blow against the British administration.*

County Down. Ballykinlar held over two thousand prisoners, who organised their own theatre companies, societies and art groups and even issued their own token coinage. The camp was referred to by its inmates as 'the university', as Frongoch had been a few years earlier.

The local elections of January 1920 — conducted under the new system of proportional representation — resulted in another comprehensive victory for Sinn Féin. Irish-American opinion was mobilised and a fund known as the Dáil Loan was extended to the United States with considerable success. The various Dáil departments continued to operate with varying degrees of effectiveness, despite surveillance. Gradually the existing judicial and local government systems crumbled or were taken over. This process, given increased momentum by the results of the 1921 election, continued up to the Treaty.

Increasingly frustrated by their failure to curb the IRA, British forces began to adopt a policy of reprisals, unofficially at first. Houses of suspected IRA members, creameries, newspaper offices, mills and whole villages were burned down by the Auxiliaries and Black and Tans as the violence escalated. On 20 September 1920 the Black and Tans burned Balbriggan in County Dublin. Other towns such as Granard, County Longford, Trim, County Meath, and Templemore, County Tipperary, were also attacked, and on 11 December the Auxiliaries burned the centre of Cork. Official reprisals, such as the burning of houses whose inhabitants 'neglected to give information to the military and police' became increasingly common, while on the other side the IRA shot informers and burned down the houses of active pro-unionists. Finally, with the military conflict in stalemate, and following preliminary negotiations, the terms of a Truce were agreed on 9 July 1921, and came into effect on 11 July.

When the Truce came into effect, British and Irish representatives commenced peace negotiations. The exclusion of a portion of Ulster, the status of the new state and the nature of the relationship with Britain, led to virtual deadlock between the Irish and British, and disagreement among the Irish themselves. Finally a Treaty was signed on 6 December 1921. After a long and angry debate in the Dáil it was ratified in January 1922, by sixty-four votes to fifty-seven. Evacuation of British regular troops,

Auxiliaries and Black and Tans commenced immediately and the RIC were disbanded. Beggars' Bush Barracks was occupied as the headquarters of the new Free State army, and by the end of May the British had evacuated most of the barracks and military installations.

In the meantime the issues that divided the pro- and anti-Treaty sides, such as the oath of allegiance to the British Crown, the status and standing of the emerging state, and partition, were exacerbated by personal antagonisms and tensions. Despite several attempted compromises — the vast majority of activists and supporters on both sides wished to avoid conflict — the country slipped towards civil war. The ensuing conflict and the bitterness that it engendered were to polarise Irish political life for generations. The basic argument, whether the Treaty was a betrayal of the Republic for which so many had given their lives, or whether it could be regarded as a stepping stone towards greater freedom, was to be settled by guns. The Civil War, from which the pro-Treaty or Free State side emerged triumphant, was indeed a sad end to a decade that had promised so much and witnessed so much idealism.

*Photo 46. Michael Collins in uniform, 1922. One of the principal organisers of the IRA, he spearheaded the undercover war against the British forces. A proponent and signatory of the Treaty, he was shot dead in an ambush during the Civil War, on 22 August 1922.*

*Photo 47. The last British guard, Dublin Castle, 1922. The castle was the headquarters of the British administration in Ireland for centuries, so the hand-over was particularly symbolic. The formal transfer of power took place on 16 January 1922.*

*Photo 48. Irish Free State troops take over Beggars' Bush Barracks, Dublin, 1922.*

*Photo 49. A contingent of the new Free State army marching across the Curragh, Co Kildare, May 1922, following the British withdrawal from Curragh Camp.*